Luxury LIFE UNVEILED

Unlocking the Secrets to Attract

Your Dream Life with No Apologies

Dr. Felisha Kay

Luxury Life Unveiled © Copyright 2024 Dr. Felisha Kay

All rights reserved. No part of this publication may be reproduced, distributed or transmitted in any form or by any means, including photocopying, recording, or other electronic or mechanical methods, without the prior written permission of the publisher, except in the case of brief quotations embodied in critical reviews and certain other noncommercial uses permitted by copyright law.

Although the author and publisher have made every effort to ensure that the information in this book was correct at press time, the author and publisher do not assume and hereby disclaim any liability to any party for any loss, damage, or disruption caused by errors or omissions, whether such errors or omissions result from negligence, accident, or any other cause.

Adherence to all applicable laws and regulations, including international, federal, state and local governing professional licensing, business practices, advertising, and all other aspects of doing business in the US, Canada, or any other jurisdiction is the sole responsibility of the reader and consumer.

Neither the author nor the publisher assumes any responsibility or liability whatsoever on behalf of the consumer or reader of this material. Any perceived slight of an individual or organization is purely unintentional.

The resources in this book are provided for informational purposes only and should not be used to replace the specialized training and professional judgment of a healthcare or a mental health professional.

Neither the author nor the publisher can be held responsible for the use of the information provided within this book. Please always consult a trained professional before making any decision regarding the treatment of yourself or others.

For more information, email contact@felishakay.com

ISBN: 979-8-9854178-0-7

Publishing Consultant:

Thanx A. Mills, LLC | www.thanxamills.com

Dynamic Dove Publishing

Table of Contents

Dedication 1

Introduction 5

Part I: The Life You Desire and Deserve 13

    Chapter 1: Unleashing Your Potential 15

    Chapter 2: The Confident Woman 29

    Chapter 3: Embracing the Luxury of Self-Care 41

Part II: The Luxury Life 55

    Chapter 4: Defining Luxury on a Deeper Level 57

    Chapter 5: Preparing For Your Luxurious Journey 65

    Chapter 6: Attracting Luxury 77

Part III: Enjoying Luxury With No Apologies 87

    Chapter 7: The Principles of Luxury 89

    Chapter 8: The Unapologetic Life 99

    Chapter 9: Embrace Your Luxurious Life 109

    Chapter 10: Luxury Life Unveiled 117

A Luxurious Love Note From The Author 121

References 123

Author Bio 127

Dedication

To my incredible daughter, Ilasiea, this book is dedicated to you, for you have illuminated my life in ways that have made me infinitely richer and more complete.

"The most important thing in your life is to be happy, to be patient, and to learn to love life and do everything you can." -**Gilles Marini**

INTRODUCTION

Have you ever wondered why you stopped dreaming? When did settling for an ordinary life become the norm? It's time to rediscover your self-worth and embrace the endless possibilities that await you.

A study conducted by the National Bureau of Economic Research reveals that nearly 80% of women struggle with low self-esteem, hindering their ability to advocate for themselves in the workplace. Individuals with low self-confidence also earn an average of $8,000 less per year than those with high self-confidence. This statistic serves as a powerful reminder of the tangible financial benefits that come with a strong sense of self-worth, as well as the potential costs of lacking it.

Luxury Life Unveiled: Unlocking the Secrets to Attract Your Dream Life with No Apologies offers a remedy to conquer self-doubt by empowering you to embrace your worthiness. It positions you to boldly attract your dream life, unrestricted by any barriers, and revel in the pleasures of living. However, this journey begins with your perception of self as you learn to embrace your true worth and value.

A person who lives a luxurious life believes they are worthy of great things with no limits and pursues life with a plan to achieve greatness. Consequently, they undoubtedly experience immense success. Yet, the person who doesn't know their worth doesn't reach the same results. It all comes down to you and the life you believe you deserve. You have the power to decide the life you want to live.

THE LUXURY LOVE DIVA

Allow me to introduce myself. My name is Dr. Felisha Kay, and I reside between the United States and Costa Rica. I have a diverse range of expertise as an Expert Luxury Love Strategist and elite Matchmaker. Cosmetic Chemist and Perfumer. My path through life has been anything but ordinary. At the age of sixteen, I embraced the role of motherhood, a responsibility that demanded strength beyond my years. Along this tumultuous journey, I found myself facing the harsh reality of homelessness, a battle that tested my resilience and resourcefulness. Moreover, I endured the horrors of domestic abuse, a dark chapter that could have consumed me entirely. However, these challenges did not shape my identity; instead, they ignited an unwavering fire, propelling my determination to triumph against all odds.

I know what it's like to feel hopeless. My abuser, who is also the father of my child, was sentenced to 75 years in prison. My daughter was only two years old, and I was 18 at the time. Shortly thereafter, I seemed to attract bad luck and horrific relationships in a six-month timeframe. I knew that something was off. I eventually realized that I was attracting the energy in which I held from within. I lacked confidence, self-value and self-worth. As a result, I attracted men who treated me poorly. I was used to being abused and disrespected for so many years, that it felt normal. Luckily it did not take me long to realized there was a pattern, so I adjusted my mindset and energy.

I was determined not to allow my two-year-old daughter to witness her mother being treated poorly by anyone. My daughter was too young to remember her father, so I set the stage for abundance early in her life and mine. I was on a mission to attract what I desired and deserved.

At 19, I started my first business, which proved to be a success, leading to its sale for an impressive sum two years later.

I had a strong desire for mentorship, so I aligned myself with people who would share wisdom and knowledge in business with me. As a result, in my early 20s, I attracted billionaire mentors. I am a firm believer that if your mentors are not among your core circle, it's ok to seek them out. Even today I appreciate mentorship and have enjoyed giving back by mentoring as well.

In 1996, I felt a strong desire to empower women to heal and rebuild, so I established one of the largest online support communities for victims and survivors of domestic violence. This groundbreaking initiative touched the lives of millions globally, earning me recognition as a recipient of the Women of Excellence Award and the prestigious title of Entrepreneur of the Year by NAFE: National Association for Female Executives. Fast forward to 2023, where I achieved another milestone by surpassing one million dollars in sales for my coaching business in its first year, earning me yet another accolade.

Many wonder how I maintain unwavering optimism and confidently embrace luxury in life and love. I have manifested a luxurious life and love, not once, but twice. I believe that I deserve the best, and want you to believe it too! I want you to experience a luxurious life because you deserve it and because it brings self-love and total freedom.

Luxury Life Unveiled: Unlocking the Secrets to Attract Your Dream Life with No Apologies

When I speak of a luxury life, I am alluding to the life you have always yearned for. It is the life you would embrace if apprehension and constraints did not hold you back. To attract this dream life, you must relinquish any reservations and self-perceptions that impede your advancement, as expounded upon within the pages of this book.

The book is divided into three sections, each guiding you towards embracing a luxurious life:

1. **Overcoming Limiting Beliefs:** The first part of this book is dedicated to helping you uncover and overcome any limiting beliefs that have been holding you back. By identifying and addressing these beliefs, you can gain the

confidence needed to pursue your dreams wholeheartedly and live a life prioritizing yourself first. No longer will you be held back by self-doubt or insecurities. Once you have built up your confidence and focus on self-care, you will realize how valuable you are.

2. **Nurturing Self-Worth:** The second section of this book is dedicated to nurturing the self-worth you cultivated in the initial section. This part will help you to identify your desires and aspirations without any hindrance from external factors. You will be free to dream big and establish ambitious objectives for yourself.

3. **Embracing a Luxurious Life:** In the final section of this book, you will embark on a transformative journey towards embracing the true essence of a luxurious life. Here, you will be equipped with the necessary tools and insights to navigate this newfound freedom and joy with confidence. No longer will you feel the need to apologize or doubt yourself, as you will possess the self-assurance to trust your instincts and make decisions that align with your desires. This final part will empower you to fully immerse yourself in the luxury and fulfillment that awaits you, leaving behind any remnants of hesitation or self-doubt.

Luxury Life Unveiled: Unlocking the Secrets to Attract Your Dream Life with No Apologies is a beacon of guidance tailored for high-performing women who desire fulfillment beyond mere success. This book is designed for hard-working professionals who may have encountered past traumas or been burdened by limiting beliefs. If you catch yourself apologizing, second-guessing, or constantly seeking validation, then this book is precisely crafted to assist you in breaking free from those detrimental patterns. It will empower you to embrace the life you've always dreamt of.

Are you ready to let go of limitations? It's time to value yourself at the highest level and attract the life you deserve.

Part I

The Life You Desire and Deserve

In this section of the book, embark on a transformative journey towards personal luxury as we explore the significance of self-belief, embracing your imperfections with grace, and nurturing the self through self-care and reflection. These chapters pave the way for a life of unapologetic luxury, where you can thrive without seeking validation from others.

Chapter 1

UNLEASHING YOUR POTENTIAL

"Once your mindset changes, everything on the outside will change along with it." -**Steve Maraboli**

Welcome to your journey towards success! I am glad you chose this book.

In life, it's important to recognize and embrace our inherent worthiness in achieving the life we truly desire. We often find ourselves held back by limiting beliefs that prevent us from believing in our potential. These beliefs can come from negative influences, self-doubt, and comparing ourselves to others. But now is the time to break free from these limitations and embrace the truth that will allow us to achieve the greatness we deserve.

Embracing What You Deserve

You are entitled to a life filled with luxury because you possess an inherent worth that deserves love, joy, triumph, contentment, and prosperity. Your value is not contingent upon external influences or the judgments of others but rather from your essence as a human being. Every individual is deserving solely by their humanity. Our intrinsic worth acknowledges the dignity and significance of every person, irrespective of their circumstances, capabilities, or perceived imperfections.

You deserve to live an amazing life because you are worthy of it. However, to experience the life you deserve, you must believe you deserve it. If your thoughts are standing in the way, then take a moment to examine why you have them, let go of the false narratives, and replace them with positive affirmations.

Understanding Limiting Beliefs

A limiting belief is a thought or state of mind that we perceive as absolute truth, which hinders us from taking specific actions. These beliefs can be about ourselves, the world, ideas, or how we interact with others. Limiting beliefs can appear in various aspects of our lives, such as doubting our physical appearance, intelligence, potential for success, impact, or ability to experience love in relationships. Whether these beliefs are inherited from others, self-imposed, or from competition, they are rooted in fear and hinder us from embracing the worthiness that we were born with. It is crucial to recognize and confront these limiting beliefs, evaluate their validity, and make changes to overcome them. By challenging and correcting these self-doubts, we can unlock our highest potential and create the luxurious life we deserve. Let's delve into the root causes of limiting beliefs.

Limiting Beliefs Imposed by Others

I label the restrictive notions imposed by others as the "you can't because" mindset. They claim you cannot pursue higher education due to financial constraints, or become a CEO because you are a woman. They even argue that you cannot enter into a new marriage because you have experienced divorce in the past.

These limitations are from others' perceptions of your worth and capabilities, but it is crucial not to allow them to shape your identity. While we overcome certain limiting beliefs imposed by others, some become ingrained in our minds, and others resurface later in life.

As accomplished women, we have faced limitations imposed on us by others. Whether it was a family member doubting our abilities or an employer suggesting we weren't ready for advancement. Sometimes, our determination to prove them wrong fueled our success, while other times, we persevered because we were driven to achieve our goals. We have all surpassed limiting beliefs imposed by others, whether it was becoming the first millionaire in our family, graduating college despite learning challenges, or exceeding others' expectations. However, the key is to eliminate all false narratives so they can't impact us later.

For example, you may have defied expectations by building a house from scratch when others doubted you. Yet, when it came time to upgrade to a larger home after doubling your salary, the negative thoughts and doubts shared with you during the first house purchase resurfaced, holding you back from pursuing your desires. Therefore, it is not enough to surpass doubts placed by others; we must recognize them and work to cancel them out so they do not hinder our future endeavors.

As accomplished women, we have proven time and again that we are capable of surpassing the limiting beliefs imposed on us by others. We have defied expectations, shattered glass ceilings, and achieved remarkable success. However, it is important to acknowledge that these external limitations can still linger within us, affecting our confidence and holding us back from reaching our full potential. By recognizing and challenging these beliefs, we can break free from their grip and continue to pursue our dreams and aspirations with unwavering determination. This empowers us to rise above the boundaries set by others and create a future where we know no limits.

SELF-IMPOSED THOUGHTS

Self-imposed limiting beliefs are the thoughts and beliefs we tell ourselves that hold us back from reaching our full potential. In the case of some women in their forties, these beliefs may revolve around appearance, such as thinking our teeth aren't straight enough, our skin is not as youthful as it used to be, or we weigh too much. These beliefs can impact our self-confidence and hinder us from pursuing our dreams or engaging in social interactions. It is crucial to love and accept ourselves unconditionally, regardless of our age or how our physical appearance may have changed over the years.

Changes in circumstances such as divorce, health, or finances can also trigger self-imposed limitations for women, leading to feelings of insecurity that can hinder our happiness. These beliefs, rooted in doubt and fear, have the potential to hold us back from finding love and pursuing fulfilling relationships. One such limiting belief that I encountered was the notion that no one would want to date or marry me because I was a single mother. This belief threatened to dampen my spirits and hinder my journey towards love and happiness. However, I made a conscious decision to overcome it by recognizing my worth.

Instead of allowing this belief to define me, I chose to love and accept myself, embracing every aspect of who I am. Through this act of self-empowerment, I gained a newfound confidence that radiated from within. As a result, I began to attract the love and support I deserved, finding a partner who not only accepted me and my daughter but cherished me for who I was. I was in my early 20's and still growing. Our marriage lasted 18 years and due to a significant age difference, we grew in opposite directions. We ultimately divorced but remain great friends.

There is life after divorce.

I never gave up on love or meeting the man that I knew was destined to find me. Shortly after my divorce, I attracted the partner I knew that I deserved. He proposed in Rome and we were married in Venice. By understanding my values and refusing to settle for anything less than what I deserve, I have been able to manifest great things in my life and loving relationships. Today, I continue to reap the benefits of this mindset, knowing that I am deserving of love, happiness, and fulfillment. It is through this journey that I have come to realize the transformative power of self-belief and the importance of recognizing and challenging the limitations we impose on ourselves. Let us all embrace our worth, break free from self-imposed limitations, and create lives filled with love, joy, and abundance.

Competition and Limitations

The notion that women don't get along with each other is a limiting belief that can hinder our collective progress. This belief often comes from a fear of not measuring up or feeling unworthy of the accomplishments and successes of other women. However, it is crucial to recognize that viewing other women as competition can hold us back from reaching our desired level of success. Instead of seeing other women's achievements as a threat, we should embrace a positive view of competition. When someone else achieves something great, it serves as evidence that we too are capable of achieving similar feats. Their success becomes a source of inspiration and motivation rather than a reason for comparison or self-doubt.

For example, imagine a determined runner sprinting with all her might, fueled by the desire to win an Olympic medal. As she races toward the finish line, she glances to her right and notices another competitor gaining ground. This competitor won the race the previous year and possessed an impressive collection of medals. At that moment, doubt creeps into the runner's mind, causing her to slow down. She believes that this experienced rival is unbeatable, and her nerves start to take hold.

Despite her doubts and hesitation, the runner completes the race but finishes second. After the race, she approaches the competitor and confesses her nervousness, admitting she didn't think she could surpass their skill and achievements. The competitor, taken aback, reveals that they were surprised to see the runner slow down. They explained that if she had maintained her initial pace, she might have emerged as the front-runner and won the medal.

This story serves as a powerful reminder of the potential hidden within us. Often, we underestimate our abilities and allow self-doubt to hinder our progress. We may compare ourselves to others, assuming they possess an insurmountable advantage. However, the truth is that we all have unique strengths and untapped potential waiting to be unleashed.

Had the runner trusted in her capabilities and continued to push forward, she might have finished in first place. This tale encourages us to believe in ourselves, embrace our strengths, and persevere even when faced with formidable competition. It reminds us that our journey is distinct and that we should never underestimate our capacity to achieve greatness.

Embracing Healthy Competition

Competition is not something to be feared. Instead of comparing ourselves to others and feeling inadequate, we should see their achievements as inspiration and set them as our next goal to achieve. For example, in the case of the runner in the above scenario, instead of thinking, "She has already won so many medals," we should adopt a mindset of "If she can do it, then so can I."

Looking at others' successes as a measure of what is possible can be empowering, but we should never doubt our capabilities. Competition reminds us of what is possible and motivates us to strive for even more extraordinary accomplishments. Networking with individuals who have achieved higher levels of success can also be beneficial, as it allows for collaboration and learning different strategies.

By shifting our mindset and embracing the idea that another woman's success does not diminish our potential, we can foster a supportive and empowering environment for all women. Together, we can celebrate each other's accomplishments, lift each other, and create a community where we all thrive. Let us break free from the limiting belief that women don't get along and instead embrace the power of collaboration and support. By recognizing that we are all entitled to achieve greatness, we can unlock our full potential and create a world where women uplift and empower each other to reach new heights of success.

How To Overcome Limiting Beliefs

To overcome doubts and limiting beliefs imposed by others or ourselves, it is important to set goals, believe in ourselves, speak life in every situation, visualize success, and be consistent.

1. Set Goals

Set clear goals and create a plan to achieve them. When negative thoughts do not align with your dreams, it is crucial to cancel them. Instead of engaging in a mental battle, it is often more effective to combat these thoughts with positive affirmations.

2. Positive Affirmations

Positive affirmations are statements that reflect your goals and aspirations positively. For example, if you are facing doubts about purchasing a bigger home, you can replace those negative thoughts with affirmations such as "I will purchase a bigger home," "The process will work out as it did before," or "I will be in my dream home soon." By repeating these affirmations, they will become more ingrained in your mind and help you visualize your desired outcome.

3. Visualization

Visualization is a powerful tool in making your dreams a reality. The more you see yourself achieving your goals and living in your dream home, the more likely you will take the necessary actions to make it a reality. Therefore, when others' negative words or doubts try to hold you back, counteract them by repeating your affirmations until you can visualize your desired outcome. As you move forward in the process, keep visualizing and affirming your goals, and you will be able to manifest your desires.

4. Consistency

Canceling doubts and limiting beliefs requires consistent effort and faith in your abilities. By replacing negative thoughts with positive affirmations and visualizing your success, you can overcome the limitations imposed by others and achieve your goals.

LIFE WITH NO LIMITS

To sum up, this chapter, recognizing and embracing our inherent worthiness is essential to creating the life we deserve. Limiting beliefs, whether self-imposed, imposed by others, or from an unhealthy view of competition, can hinder us from reaching our full potential. We deserve a luxurious life filled with love, happiness, success, and abundance. Our worth is not determined by external factors or the opinions of others but by our inherent value as human beings. By believing in ourselves, setting goals, using positive affirmations, visualizing success, and being consistent, we can overcome limiting beliefs and achieve the greatness we deserve. It is time to break free from the shackles of self-doubt and embrace the truth that we are worthy of everything beautiful life has to offer.

Chapter 2

THE CONFIDENT WOMAN

*"Too many people overvalue what they are not and undervalue what they are." -**Malcolm S. Forbes***

In the initial chapter, we discussed how every individual has the right to experience greatness in their life. This means that abundance is our birthright and we deserve it in every aspect of our existence. However, this abundance can only come to fruition once we overcome our limiting beliefs and develop the confidence to pursue our desires. This chapter focuses on the importance of valuing oneself at the highest level through the power of confidence.

Confidence is the unwavering belief and trust in oneself and one's abilities. It means being self-assured and having faith in our skills, knowledge, and qualities. When we are confident, we feel empowered to face challenges, take calculated risks, and believe in our potential for success. Confidence is linked to maintaining a positive mindset, being assertive, and having a strong sense of self-worth.

To better understand confidence, let's break it down into two aspects: confidence in life and confidence in love. It's important to differentiate between the two because a person can be confident in themselves but lack confidence in their relationships with others.

CONFIDENCE IN LIFE

Have you ever observed someone at a networking event who appears uncomfortable and out of place? They may be scanning the room, trying to meet as many people as possible, but their awkwardness is evident because they are not being true to themselves. This is not a confident person. This is someone who is still unsure of how to show up authentically.

Confidence in life involves being comfortable with who you are, embracing your strengths and weaknesses, and accepting yourself as a whole. It means being authentic to yourself, without seeking validation or approval from others.

Confidence in life is not about pretending to be someone you're not. It's not about trying to fit in or impress others. True confidence comes from knowing and embracing who you are at all times and not being afraid to shine.

WHAT CONFIDENCE IN LIFE IS NOT

1. **Never Having Limiting Beliefs-** Confidence is not about never doubting yourself. It means having a plan and a goal to counter negative thoughts with positive affirmations. By consistently speaking life into yourself, you can maintain a confident mindset.
2. **Not having fear-** Confidence entails working through fear. It means evaluating situations logically and distinguishing between what is real and what is not. By

doing so, you can overcome fear and move forward with confidence.

3. **Always Feeling Secure-** Confidence in life doesn't mean you will always feel your best. It's about maintaining a positive attitude and believing that everything will work out for you. It means working through challenges with optimism and gratitude and trusting the process of your journey.

4. **Being silent or combative-** A confident person knows when to speak and not. This is someone who has wisdom and will not argue with people who don't have the same understanding or beliefs and who also will not remain silent when they have answers and solutions to help others. Confidence is knowing when the time is right to make a difference for others.

5. **Avoiding Confrontations or disagreements-** Confidence in life doesn't mean avoiding healthy challenges from others. It means never allowing the words, thoughts, or actions of others to determine your worth. It means not being desperate, needy, or seeking constant acceptance and validation. Instead, it involves being comfortable with validating yourself, even if those

around you may not necessarily share your views. It is okay to agree to disagree.

It's important not to confuse confidence in life without recognizing there will still be challenges. Confidence when it comes to life means you are certain that you will make the right choices, use wisdom, and that you possess what it takes to do whatever you desire.

Confidence in Love and Relationships

Confidence in love encompasses the ability to engage in both personal and business relationships while valuing oneself. It goes beyond self-love and self-acceptance, extending to the understanding that the love we give to others is only as strong as the love we have for ourselves. This love should be unwavering and unconditional. With confidence, we establish standards and boundaries in relationships, having high expectations to be loved, appreciated, and respected by those around us.

A Tale of Confidence (or Lack Thereof)

While engrossed in a dating reality show, I couldn't help but notice a recurring pattern among some of the women seeking love. They would pour out their hopes and dreams to a man they had just met, only to have him deceitfully mold himself into the person they desired. These women would feel betrayed and hurt when the true man finally showed up and they could see how the person was.

Confidence in love is not about desperately seeking validation from others. It is about recognizing that we are already complete and fulfilled as individuals. We don't need a partner to define us; we are already successful in our own right.

This concept extends beyond personal relationships and applies to business partnerships as well. Confidence is not about hastily joining forces with someone based solely on emotions. It involves conducting thorough research and ensuring alignment and compatibility. Without shared goals and values, it is impossible to achieve success together. Confidence in love means trusting others while also holding them accountable.

Now, let's discuss what confidence in love is not.

WHAT CONFIDENCE IN LOVE IS NOT

1. Confidence in love is not about people-pleasing. It is about recognizing when our confidence and dignity are being compromised and having the strength to walk away

from such situations. It means standing up for ourselves and prioritizing our well-being.

2. Confidence in love is not about oversharing our hopes and dreams with just anyone. True confidence lies in knowing who to trust and confide in. It means surrounding ourselves with supportive and trustworthy individuals who uplift and encourage us.

3. Confidence in love is not about turning a blind eye to red flags or pursuing something solely based on emotions. It involves being aware of inconsistencies and addressing them rather than ignoring them.

4. Confidence in love is not about being one-sided in relationships, constantly giving without receiving. True confidence involves maintaining a healthy balance and understanding the importance of reciprocity.

5. Confidence in love is not about despising solitude. It is about embracing and cherishing our own company. It means finding joy and fulfillment in spending time with ourselves and being comfortable in our skin.

A confident person loves every aspect of themselves, including their flaws and weaknesses. They work on what they can change and accept what they cannot. They find security within themselves, not relying on validation from others.

In conclusion, confidence in love is not about compromising our well-being or seeking validation from others. It is not about sharing our dreams with those who may not have our best interests at heart. It is not about ignoring red flags or being one-sided in relationships. And it is certainly not about fearing solitude, but rather finding contentment and happiness within ourselves.

Manifestation

We have discussed what we deserve, overcoming limiting beliefs, and how to be confident in life and love. Now let's explore how to manifest the confidence we need and prevent old beliefs from holding us back through manifestation.

Manifestation is a powerful tool that allows us to bring into our lives what we truly desire and deserve. It involves using our thoughts, beliefs, and intentions to attract or create desired outcomes or experiences. By focusing on what we want and believing in its possibilities, we can manifest our desires into reality. Here are some steps to help you manifest what you want:

1. **Define your desires**: Take the time to identify and clarify what you truly want. Be specific and clear about what you want to manifest in your life. Visualize it, feel it, and believe that it is already yours.
2. **Set intentions**: Write down your intentions and create affirmations to reinforce them. Use visualization techniques, such as creating a vision board, to focus your energy and have a clear picture of what you desire.
3. **Alignment**: Examine your thoughts and beliefs about deserving what you desire. Let go of any limiting beliefs or self-doubt that may be holding you back. Replace them with positive affirmations and beliefs that support your worthiness and the manifestation of your desires.
4. **Take action:** Manifestation requires taking inspired action towards your goals. Listen to your intuition and take steps that align with your desires. Let peace guide you towards the right opportunities and resources.
5. **Gratitude**: Practice gratitude for what you already have as you expect your future desires to come. Express gratitude daily through journaling, affirmations, and acknowledging the blessings in your life. Gratitude amplifies positive energy and attracts more of what you desire.

6. **Trust the process**: Let go of attachment to the outcome and trust that you will receive what you deserve at the perfect time. Have faith that what is meant for you will come to you.

7. **Expect great things:** Be open to receiving the manifestations of your desires. Pay attention to synchronicities, signs, and opportunities that come your way. Trust your intuition and follow the guidance that arises.

Remember, manifesting what you desire is a journey that requires patience, belief, and consistent effort. Trust in your worthiness and the power of manifestation. By aligning your thoughts, beliefs, and actions with your desires, you can manifest the life you truly deserve with confidence.

HIGH-VALUE CONFIDENCE

To restate this second chapter, confidence is key to living a luxurious life and attracting what you desire. With confidence, we can manifest the life we truly deserve. It is through the power of confidence that we can value ourselves at the highest level and pursue our desires with unwavering belief and trust from within. Confidence in life means being comfortable with who we are, embracing our strengths and weaknesses, and accepting ourselves as a whole. It means being authentic to ourselves, without seeking validation or approval from others.

Confidence in love and relationships extends beyond self-love and self-acceptance. It involves recognizing that we are already complete and fulfilled as individuals, and we don't need a partner to define us. Confidence in love means establishing standards and boundaries and expecting to be loved, appreciated, and respected by those around us. It means trusting others while also holding them accountable and ensuring alignment and compatibility in relationships.

To manifest the confidence, we need and prevent old beliefs from holding us back, we can utilize the power of manifestation. By defining our desires, setting intentions, aligning our thoughts and beliefs, taking inspired action, practicing gratitude, trusting the process, and expecting great things, we can manifest our desires into reality.

Remember, manifesting what we deserve is a journey that requires patience, belief, and consistent effort. But with confidence as our guiding force, we can overcome any obstacles and create the life we truly desire. So let us embrace our worthiness, trust in ourselves, and manifest our dreams with confidence.

Chapter 3

EMBRACING THE LUXURY OF SELF-CARE

"Love yourself first and everything else falls in line. You really have to love yourself to get anything done in this world." -**Lucille Ball**

Do you ever quickly shower, dry off, and collapse into bed? If so, then are you truly treating yourself as the high-value person you are?

Now that we have explored the importance of confidence and understanding our worth, it is time to shift our focus to the concept of self-care and its vital role in ensuring our minds and bodies are prepared to experience the luxury they deserve. This chapter explores the concepts of how valuable we are, self-care, boundaries, and consistently taking care of our physical, mental, and emotional aspects of living so that we can be prepared to live and sustain a luxurious life.

VALUE

Not everything holds the same level of significance in our lives. When we value something, we treat it with special care and attention. For instance, I have a collection of jewelry. While each piece may be beautiful, there is one that holds immense sentimental value, which is my wedding ring. I keep it in a special place and treat it differently because of its high importance to me.

Similarly, we should prioritize and value our own lives above all else. Our lives are the foundation upon which everything else is built, and without a strong sense of value in self, we cannot contribute to, or benefit the lives of others. So, how can we demonstrate the value we place on our lives? Self-care is the best way to make sure you preserve yourself. Engaging in self-care is a powerful way to show appreciation for the worth and significance of our lives.

SELF-CARE

Self-care is an essential aspect of embracing a luxurious life. Self-care deliberately nurtures our physical, emotional, and mental well-being, allowing us to bask in relaxation, self-compassion, and personal growth. Practicing self-care is not an act of selfishness but rather a testament to our self-worth and the recognition of our deserving nature. Just as we handle luxurious possessions with care and admiration, we must treat ourselves with even more gentleness and attention. Once we take care of ourselves, then we can create a luxurious life by not only loving and doing good for ourselves but also doing good and helping others.

BOUNDARIES

When I host dinner parties or gatherings at my house, my family and friends are well aware that I value punctuality. Time is an important factor in my planning, and I organize everything accordingly. As a result, I rarely have people showing up late and disrupting the flow of the event without giving prior notice or a call. It is understood that I plan based on a specific number of guests and allocate time accordingly, so they are also mindful to RSVP.

I have established a clear boundary and standard regarding punctuality for events I host, and I never feel the need to apologize for it. It is important to me that everyone respects the time and effort I put into planning, and I appreciate when guests adhere to the agreed-upon schedule. By setting this boundary, I ensure that my guests can fully enjoy the gathering without any disruptions or delays. Therefore, my commitment to punctuality is a boundary that I have set and maintained. It is a standard that I hold dear, and I firmly believe that it contributes to the overall enjoyment and smooth running of the events I host.

Implementing boundaries in our relationships empowers those around us to reflect on their behavior and make positive changes in how they interact with us and others. By establishing clear expectations for kindness and respect, we set a standard that others must meet to be a part of our lives. This not only teaches them how to treat us but also encourages them to treat others with the same level of respect.

Do you have clear boundaries in your relationships? Boundaries play a vital role in our relationships and overall well-being. They are an essential aspect of self-care that allows us to live a luxurious life without feeling the need to apologize for it. By setting and maintaining healthy boundaries, we prioritize our emotional, mental, and physical health, leading to more meaningful connections with others.

Emotional Boundaries

Emotional boundaries are essential for prioritizing our feelings and needs, preventing emotional exhaustion, and cultivating healthy relationships. It is vital to recognize and address anything that bothers us, voice our concerns, and avoid situations that can be draining and stressful. In relationships, it is especially important to communicate our displeasure, as others may not be aware of how their actions affect us. By establishing clear boundaries on what we are willing to accept and what we are not, we assert our self-worth and demand respect and love from others.

It is important to remember that boundaries are not fixed and can evolve as we grow and transform. What may have been acceptable to us in the past may no longer align with our values and needs, and that is perfectly okay. For instance, if a friend becomes a vegetarian due to ethical reasons, it would be inappropriate to invite them to an all-you-can-eat meat buffet, as it disregards their boundaries. Emotional boundaries not only protect our own emotions but also respect the boundaries of others.

By establishing and maintaining emotional boundaries, we create a space where our emotions are valued and protected. This allows us to nurture our well-being and build healthier, more fulfilling relationships based on mutual respect and understanding.

MENTAL BOUNDARIES

Mental boundaries play a crucial role in safeguarding our mental health by regulating the information and stimuli we allow into our minds. For instance, it is important to be mindful of the timing and content of the news we consume. Watching distressing news right before bed can disrupt our sleep and negatively impact our mental well-being. Similarly, reaching for our cell phones immediately upon waking can bombard us with external influences before we have had a chance to prepare ourselves mentally for the day ahead. By consciously creating a peaceful mental environment, we protect our well-being. This empowers us to make choices that are authentic to our true selves, unaffected by external factors. By setting boundaries around our mental space, we cultivate a sense of clarity, focus, and inner peace, allowing us to navigate life with intention and alignment.

Physical Boundaries

Setting physical boundaries involves placing limits on our energy, time, and resources. Many individuals prioritize their physical well-being by dedicating time in the morning to activities like walking or running. By taking care of their bodies first, they set a foundation for their overall mental and emotional health. One way I establish physical boundaries is by activating the "do not disturb" mode on my phone when I indulge in a massage. This allows me to fully immerse myself in the experience and pay attention to any part of my body that may need extra care. Recognizing the significance of time and rest not only helps prevent physical and mental exhaustion but also creates space for personal growth and enjoyment. When we value our well-being with physical boundaries, we demonstrate that self-care is not selfish but essential to balance and sustain our lives.

In essence, boundaries serve as a powerful tool that allows us to unconditionally cherish our physical, mental, and emotional well-being. By embracing boundaries as a form of self-care without any apologies, we tap into our inner strength and cultivate a life filled with joy, fulfillment, and meaningful connections. Ultimately, this creates a ripple effect of positive change in our relationships and the lives of those around us.

CONSISTENT SELF-CARE ROUTINES

Treating our bodies as a luxury is not just reserved for special occasions. It is a daily practice that allows us to recognize our worth and attract the abundance and opulence that we deserve. By consistently taking the time to care for our physical bodies, mentally and emotionally, we will be in a position to attract a life of luxury that aligns with our true values. Self-care is a personal journey, so it's important to find what works best for you.

SELF-CARE FOR OUR PHYSICAL BODIES

Treat yourself like royalty. Here are some ways to perform self-care for your body to signify your body's high-value level:

1. **Regular Health Check-ups:** Schedule regular check-ups with your healthcare provider to monitor your overall

health and address any concerns or preventive measures. This includes your annual physical, mammogram, dentist, vision, and any other specialized visit. Be sure to keep a record of your appointments and do any necessary follow-ups.

2. **Prioritize Hygiene:** Not rushing through showers and going to bed, but being mindful to cleanse your body, brush your teeth and floss, and moisturize your skin. This helps keep your body fresh and healthy.

3. **Nutrition & Hydration:** Our body requires a balanced diet that includes fruits, vegetables, proteins, and healthy fats. Drink plenty of water throughout the day to keep your body hydrated and functioning and limit your sugar intake.

4. **Get Regular Exercise:** Engage in physical activity that you enjoy, such as walking, jogging, dancing, or yoga. I happen to love pilates! Exercise is also proven to positively affect our mental health. Regular exercise helps improve cardiovascular health, strength, flexibility, and overall well-being.

5. **Prioritize Sleep:** Plan your rest just as you set aside time for everything else. Establish a consistent sleep routine and aim for 7-9 hours of quality sleep each night. Create a

relaxing bedtime routine and ensure your sleep environment is comfortable and conducive to rest.

6. **Listen to Your Body:** Pay attention to any discomfort or pain in your body and address it promptly. Do not ignore warning signs. Rest when needed and seek medical attention if necessary.

7. **Relaxation and Stress Management:** Engage in activities that help you relax and manage stress, such as deep breathing exercises, meditation, or taking breaks throughout the day to rest and recharge. Consider having a cup of herbal tea to relieve tension.

Remember, self-care for your body is about nourishing and respecting it. Listen to your body's needs, be kind to yourself, and make choices that promote your physical well-being.

SELF-CARE FOR MENTAL & EMOTIONAL STRENGTH

Taking care of our mental and emotional health is just as important as caring for our physical well-being. Here are some ways to perform self-care for your mental and emotional health:

1. **Practice Mindfulness and Meditation:** Set aside time each day to practice mindfulness or meditation. This can

help calm your mind, reduce stress, and increase self-awareness.

2. **Engage in Activities You Enjoy:** Participate in activities that bring you joy and help you relax, such as reading, listening to music, painting, or engaging in hobbies. These activities can provide a sense of fulfillment and help you unwind.

3. **Prioritize Self-Compassion:** Be kind and understanding towards yourself. Practice self-compassion by acknowledging your feelings, accepting imperfections, and treating yourself with the same kindness you would offer to a loved one.

4. **Seek Support:** Reach out to trusted friends, family members, or professionals when you need support. Talking about your feelings and concerns can provide comfort and perspective. However, keeping things inside creates internal pain that affects you in other ways. Therapists, counselors, or mental health professionals can also provide guidance, support, and tools to help you navigate challenges.

5. **Set Boundaries:** As we mentioned earlier in this chapter, boundaries are crucial. Establish healthy boundaries in your relationships and learn to say no when necessary.

This helps protect your mental and emotional well-being by ensuring that you have time and energy for self-care.

6. **Limit Exposure to Negative Influences:** Be mindful of the media, social media, the news, and negative environments that can impact your mental and emotional health. Set boundaries around your consumption and prioritize positive and uplifting content.

7. **Practice Self-Reflection:** Take time to reflect on your thoughts, emotions, and experiences. Journaling or engaging in self-reflection exercises can help you gain insight, process emotions, and foster personal growth.

Remember, self-care for your mental and emotional health is an ongoing practice. It's important to prioritize your well-being, be patient with yourself, and seek help when needed.

EMBRACE SELF-CARE

To summarize the main points discussed in this chapter, self-care, setting boundaries, and consistently taking care of our physical, mental, and emotional well-being are crucial for living a fulfilling and abundant life. By prioritizing self-care and treating ourselves as luxuries, we can boost our confidence, recognize our self-worth, and attract abundance into our lives. Let's cultivate a sense of appreciation and care for our bodies, treating them with love and respect. This daily practice allows us to live a life of luxury and enjoy the opulence we deserve.

PART II

THE LUXURY LIFE

In the upcoming chapters, I will discuss the essence of luxury, unravel its true meaning, explore the art of preparing for it, and ultimately, describe how to magnetize its presence into your lives.

Chapter 4

DEFINING LUXURY ON A DEEPER LEVEL

"Value yourself at the highest level in life and in love."
-*Dr. Felisha Kay*

Last year, I carefully made my bed, and my curious daughter stood nearby and said, *"Wow, your bed looks so luxurious!"* I couldn't help but agree, proudly stating that my entire room exudes luxury. She then said, *"Mom everything that you touch seems to exude luxury. I have many memories from when I was a child, you always made everything feel special, or shall I say, luxurious!"* It was then that I explained to her that luxury is not limited to a physical location but rather a state of mind. I emphasized that when we perceive things as luxurious, they become just that in our eyes. To my delight, she nodded in agreement. This story serves as a reminder that we can live a life of luxury regardless of our circumstances. A large ten-acre estate is not a prerequisite for luxury; even a modest apartment can be considered luxurious if we choose to see it that way. By adopting this mindset, we naturally treat our living space with the utmost care and attention to detail. We ensure it remains spotless, free of broken items, and decorate it with simple yet elegant touches that don't break the bank. For instance, investing $300 in a matching comforter set with a high thread count can instantly transform a bedroom and sleep into luxury. Ultimately, luxury as a state of mind means recognizing our worth and attributing the high value to the things around us.

THREE TYPES OF LUXURY

Luxury is about desiring more and aligning ourselves with the life we have always dreamed of. I often say that attracting abundance is an inside job. It requires a combination of mindset shifts, actions, steps, and habits that align with our goals.

I will define luxury on a deeper level and break it down into three parts: luxury as a material thing, luxury as a feeling, and what it means to embody luxury as a person.

LUXURY ITSELF

Luxury is associated with high quality, comfort, exclusivity, and extravagance. It encompasses products, services, or experiences considered superior or premium compared to their standard counterparts. Luxury experiences can range from staying at a modern five-star hotel to chartering a private jet for a dream vacation. These experiences provide a sense of indulgence and offer an escape from the ordinary. However, the perception of luxury can be subjective and varies from person to person and across different cultures.

I once watched a game show where Kelly Ripa was the host, and a family had to choose between winning a new BMW car or a beautiful dollhouse. The decision was left to the youngest family member, a little girl, who couldn't hear the crowd's opinions due to the noise-canceling headphones placed over her ears. It made me chuckle, as an eight-year-old girl might desire a Barbie dream house, while as a grown woman, a luxury BMW would be in a league of its own. However, the concept of luxury evolves as we grow and change. At sixteen, you may be content with a car passed down from your parents, but as you get older, you may aspire to own a brand-new vehicle. The key is to determine what things are luxury to you personally. Don't let others' opinions or societal expectations dictate what you should consider luxurious, as it may not align with your current desires. It is essential to define what luxury things and experiences are important to you based on your values and beliefs.

Luxury Feeling

The feeling of luxury is indeed based on how you feel about yourself and your life. It is a sense of freedom that comes from within and is not reliant on external factors like wealth or status. Luxury is about being able to express yourself authentically, pursue your passions without fear or limitation, and live a fulfilling life that aligns with your values and beliefs.

In the example of the little girl with noise-canceling headphones, it is good to cancel out the opinions of others and determine what luxury feels like to you personally. Just as the little girl chose the beautiful dollhouse with a big grin, it is crucial to pursue your passions. Going after things that matter to others but not to yourself will not bring you the true luxury feeling that you deserve. Thus, follow your heart and cancel out the noise from those around you.

Imagine how you feel when walking into a beautiful suite. You're immediately enveloped in an atmosphere of refined elegance, where every detail, from the plush carpets to the artfully arranged decor, speaks of quality and sophistication. The air carries a subtle, soothing scent, and the soft, ambient lighting creates a serene oasis that whispers of comfort and indulgence. You immediately feel a sense of luxury.

Another aspect of luxury feelings is how you perceive your beauty. Your beauty should not be determined by magazines or societal standards. Instead, it is up to you to define what looks and feels beautiful. Beauty is in the eye of the beholder, and different people have different preferences. Some may prefer thinner individuals, while others prefer a more voluptuous figure. Some may like natural hair over wigs. It is important to be your judge of beauty and decide what feels right to you. Remember, true beauty comes from within.

In summary, luxury feelings are about how you feel about yourself and your life. It's the feeling you have when in a luxury environment like a suite. The feeling of luxury is also about the freedom to express yourself authentically and pursue your passions without limitations. It is important to cancel out the opinions of others and follow your desires. Additionally, you should define your beauty based on what looks and feels nice. Embrace your uniqueness and remember that true beauty comes from within.

Luxury Person

Lastly, let's explore the concept of embodying luxury as a person. While luxury itself is associated with material possessions and experiences, it is also possible to embody luxury as a personal trait or characteristic. In this context, luxury can be seen as someone who consistently exudes elegance, refinement, and sophistication in all aspects of their life.

A person who embodies luxury may have an impeccable sense of fashion, a deep appreciation for art and culture, and a preference for the finer things in life. They surround themselves with beauty and quality, and their choices reflect a refined taste. Additionally, they possess a certain grace and poise that sets them apart from others. However, it is imperative to understand that embodying luxury does not imply a sense of superiority.

A truly luxurious person not only possesses style and class but also demonstrates kindness, generosity, and humility towards others. When they enter a room, people are naturally drawn to their presence like a sparkling gemstone. They understand that true luxury lies not only in material possessions but also in how they treat and uplift those around them. A luxurious person leaves a lasting impression not just through their appearance or demeanor but also through the warmth and positivity they bring into people's lives.

In essence, embodying luxury as a person means combining style, class, and character. It involves living life with intentionality and purpose while appreciating the beauty and richness of the world. A luxurious person understands that true luxury goes beyond external appearances.

The Luxury Suite, Things, Feelings, Embodiment

As we discussed, luxury can be things, feelings, and the embodiment of a person. Luxury, in the context of one's life, encompasses more than just material possessions or external experiences. It is a deeply personal and subjective concept beyond wealth or status. Luxury is about the feeling it evokes within oneself: a sense of indulgence, comfort, and exclusivity. It is about embodying luxury, carrying oneself with confidence and authenticity, and pursuing passions and desires without limitations. Luxury is about aligning one's life with one's values and beliefs, prioritizing experiences and possessions that bring a sense of fulfillment and joy. It is about creating a lifestyle that reflects one's definition of luxury, free from outside noise or societal expectations. Luxury is a state of mind, and a way of living that enhances overall well-being and personal growth.

Chapter 5

PREPARING FOR YOUR LUXURIOUS JOURNEY

"Never settle for anything less than what you deserve, it's not pride, it's self-respect." - **Mind Blood**

In the previous chapter, we discussed the concept of luxury and how it can be defined by our personal experiences and feelings. Now, let's embark on a journey to attain a luxury-filled life.

The first step in preparing for this journey is to establish a clear goal for the luxurious lifestyle we desire. Next, we must identify and overcome any obstacles hindering our progress. Finally, we should envision a life where we can pursue our desires without fear or hesitation. Let's explore each step.

Our Luxury Desires

The first step to preparing for luxury is to determine what it means to us. We aim to encompass all aspects of luxury, including feelings, possessions, and being a person who exudes luxury. We must strive for a life that aligns with this three-part definition of luxury. Let's delve into each part of luxury to be clear on what we want.

Luxury Feelings

In our journey through life, we are often taught to analyze and make rational decisions. But what if we started making choices based on what feels right? This approach not only helps us understand our instincts but also enables us to trust our intuition. After all, no one else can dictate how we should feel or what we should seek. What do you think when you see children? How do you feel about the weather or politics? How do you believe in general? It is crucial to follow what feels right to you, especially when it comes to your pursuit of luxury, rather than conforming to expectations or relying solely on logical reasoning.

This principle holds particular significance in relationships. Instead of choosing a partner out of fear of being alone or because others believe you make a great couple, opt for someone who genuinely feels right when you are in their presence. Look for someone whose conversations and perspectives resonate with you rather than making you cringe. While they say opposites attract, it is essential to note that if a person holds opposing beliefs and values, it may not feel right for you. Take the time to identify your feelings about what luxury means to you and the kind of life you desire. Do not allow external influences to seep into your decision-making process.

By focusing on your feelings, you create a space that pushes away the opinions of others and helps you overcome any limiting beliefs that may try to resurface. This emphasis on your own emotions empowers you to conquer any obstacles that stand in the way of your pursuit of true luxury.

Luxury Itself (Things)

Regarding luxury itself, it is essential to consider the things and experiences that truly matter to you. Luxury is not about being in places you don't want to be. You define the luxury things you want. It is about embracing high quality, comfort, exclusivity, and extravagance that align with your preferences. Do you desire to explore new destinations through travel? Or perhaps investing in real estate is what resonates with you. Your luxury choices should be based on your values, as this will ultimately impact how you feel.

To prepare for luxury, we have to determine what specific things and experiences hold importance to us. For example, I had a friend who believed that traveling the world was the ultimate definition of a luxurious life. However, my description of luxury centered on building wealth, acquiring assets, and being debt-free. Therefore, at that time, traveling was not a priority for me. While my friend was jet-setting across the globe, I focused on growing my financial portfolio. Both paths represented luxury, but they were different because we had distinct priorities. Therefore, you should carefully decide on the things and experiences that genuinely align with your values and aspirations.

Luxury as a Person (Embodiment)

Being a person of luxury entails having a profound sense of self-worth and confidence not just style and elegance. It involves recognizing one's value and treating oneself with utmost respect and dignity. A luxury person understands the significance of self-care and places importance on their physical, mental, and emotional well-being above their image.

It is important to note that the concept of a luxury person is subjective, as it is based on one's desire to embody luxury. To me, a luxury person comprehends that true luxury lies in creating meaningful memories and forging connections. They are mindful and aware of their impact on the world. They make ethical choices and support causes and organizations that align with their values, actively working towards making a positive difference in the world.

A luxury person is also someone who embraces diversity and inclusivity. They celebrate and respect individuals from all walks of life, regardless of their background, race, gender, or beliefs. They understand the significance of empathy and compassion, striving to create a world where everyone feels valued and accepted. I love to leave a room filled with people who feel uplifted for having met me because of the way I made them feel.

The above description represents my interpretation of a person who embodies luxury, but it is perfectly acceptable if your perspective differs. As you define the luxury person you aspire to be, remember that being a luxury person means being an example that others want to emulate. It involves embodying kindness, and forgiveness, and displaying love, joy, and character for others to strive towards. If we find ourselves lacking any of the qualities necessary to achieve our goal of embodying luxury, then we must let go of those shortcomings.

LETTING GO

The next step in preparing for luxury is getting rid of the things that aren't beneficial. Now that we know the luxury we desire, let's get rid of any hindrances. Two main things that hold people back from experiencing luxury are limiting beliefs and unforgiveness. As discussed in Chapter One, limiting beliefs are negative thoughts or beliefs we hold about ourselves or the world around us. These beliefs can be deeply ingrained and often go unnoticed, but they can significantly impact our lives by holding us back from achieving our full potential. However, by identifying and challenging these beliefs, we can begin to shift our mindset towards one of empowerment and visualize the possibilities.

In addition to overcoming limiting beliefs and keeping them behind us, forgiveness is also essential. Forgiveness is a powerful tool that helps us attract a life of luxury. Holding onto grudges and resentments creates negative energy that blocks positive things from entering our lives. By practicing forgiveness and letting go of past hurts, we free ourselves from this negative energy and open ourselves up to new opportunities and abundance.

Forgiveness involves having an open heart and mind letting go of anger and bitterness towards those who have wronged us. It's important to understand that holding onto these negative emotions only harms us in the long run. By choosing to forgive, we release ourselves from these negative feelings, creating space for positive energy to flow into our lives and attract more good things.

Forgiveness also helps us cultivate compassion and empathy towards others, attracting positive relationships. Approaching others with kindness and understanding creates a positive energy that draws people towards us. Moreover, forgiveness removes mental barriers that may be holding us back, allowing us to move forward with confidence and clarity.

REIMAGINE YOUR FABULOUS SELF

Now that you have defined your luxurious life and agreed to be free of limitations and unforgiveness, reimagining your fabulous self is the next step in preparation for a luxurious life.

Reimagining a new version of ourselves, our most fabulous selves, is empowering and transformative.

It involves envisioning the person we aspire to be, letting go of self-imposed limitations, and embracing our unique strengths and talents. This process requires seeing ourselves as confident, accomplished, and fulfilled individuals and taking action to make that vision a reality.

To begin, we should identify the aspects we want to change or improve. Whether it's gaining more confidence, compassion, health, or a sense of adventure, we should allow ourselves to dream big and envision the best possible version of ourselves. Taking small steps towards that vision, trying new things, setting goals, and practicing positive self-talk is key.

Visualization is a powerful tool for reimagining ourselves. By visualizing ourselves as the person we want to become, living the life we've always dreamed of, and embodying our desired qualities, we can manifest our dreams. Visualization helps in cultivating a mindset of positivity and possibility.

Reimagining ourselves doesn't mean erasing who we are now; it's about a fundamental transformation within us. It's about unlocking our true potential, discovering our purpose, and living authentically.

Reimagining ourselves is not just about positive evolution but also about embracing a Luxury Mindset. A Luxury Mindset is the belief that our qualities and essence can be polished and refined through deliberate effort, commitment, and embracing every experience as an opulent lesson. It's about viewing challenges as avenues for personal enrichment rather than hindrances to be sidestepped. I see it as an avenue to relentless self-enhancement.

To help reimagine yourself and access your zenith of potential, consider these refined strategies:

1. **Nurture a Luxury Mindset:** Adopt an open-minded stance towards personal development and refinement.

Believe in your capacity to evolve and elevate your character and persona over time.

2. **Embrace your strengths:** Recognize your unique qualities and deepen their enhancement. This not only bolsters your self-assurance but also imparts a sense of self-worth and purpose.

3. **Take intentional steps:** Make deliberate, refined choices that align with your goals each day. Realize that true elegance and class are the products of consistent effort and are not instantaneously realized.

4. **Surround yourself with refinement:** Engage with individuals who inspire and elevate you. Distance yourself from negativity or those who might stifle your pursuit of elegance.

5. **Prioritize self-indulgence:** Allocate time for your physical, emotional, and mental nourishment. By pampering yourself, you alleviate stress and augment your overall contentment and satisfaction.

6. **Celebrate your milestones:** When you attain a goal or progress towards your envisioned life, toast to your accomplishments. Use these moments as momentum to carry you forward.

7. **Seek tailored advice:** Don't be hesitant to approach mentors, connoisseurs, or anyone who can offer precious insights and guidance as you journey toward your aspirations.
8. **Foster gratitude:** Concentrate on the luxurious aspects of your life and show appreciation for them daily. This change in mindset towards abundance will magnetize further opulence into your life.

By adopting these strategies, you can embark on a transformative voyage of self-enhancement and sophistication. Remember, reimagining ourselves is not a mere endpoint but a continuous odyssey of sculpting the finest version of ourselves.

Your Luxurious Journey

In essence, adopting a Luxury Mindset means setting definitive aspirations, navigating challenges with grace, and envisioning our lives enveloped in opulence. As we embark on this sophisticated journey, let's approach it with receptive hearts and discerning minds. Armed with resolve and tenacity, we are poised to indulge in the true essence of a luxurious existence.

Chapter 6

ATTRACTING LUXURY

"The longer you entertain what's not for you, the longer you postpone what is." – **Kayla Simone**

We discussed that you deserve abundance because you are a human being so it's your birthright. We also discussed how to overcome limiting beliefs to dream and desire great things as well as the different forms of luxury for you to determine the luxurious life that you want. Now we will discuss how to attract the luxury you desire.

LAW OF ATTRACTION

Early on we discussed manifestation. Manifestation is the process of bringing your desires, goals, and dreams into reality through focused intention and positive thinking. It involves harnessing the power of your mind and emotions to attract and create the experiences and outcomes that you want in your life. The idea behind manifestation is that we create our reality with our thoughts and beliefs, and by aligning them with our goals, we can bring those goals to fruition.

Manifestation can involve various practices, including visualization, affirmations, gratitude, and meditation, which help to align your thoughts, beliefs, and actions with your desired outcomes. By focusing on what you want, rather than what you don't want, and maintaining an optimistic mindset, you can bring about the manifestation of your goals and dreams.

The law of attraction is a powerful tool that helps to manifest your desires by focusing on positive energy and thought, visualizing your ideal future, and taking consistent action towards achieving your goals. It works by believing in yourself and your capability to attract abundance and success into your life. By using the power of the law of attraction, you can create a life filled with happiness and fulfillment.

ATTRACTING YOUR DREAM LIFE

Now I'll share some of the things I have been able to manifest and the abundance that I have attracted in life and love.

Throughout my life, I have been able to manifest abundance and attract incredible experiences in both my personal and professional life. I attribute this to using the DIVA Model, which I will explain in more detail later in this chapter.

From a young age, I possessed the ability to dream big and attract what I desired. My parents, both of my grandmothers, and many family and friends always saw me as fearless, loving, kind, and curious, and they believed that I would be blessed because of these qualities.

I mentioned at the age of 19, I started my first successful business, which was a house cleaning company. I needed a job so I cleaned houses for a big company. When I realized what they were making, and I was doing all of the work, I decided to start my own business. It was a huge success!

In my early 20s, I had the privilege of attracting billionaire mentors who guided me on my journey. I made a conscious effort to align myself with individuals who could help me achieve my goals.

Driven by my passion, I fulfilled my dream of becoming a beauty chemist and an internationally trained perfumer. Along the way, I surrounded myself with top industry leaders who became not only mentors but also personal friends.

When my 18-year marriage ended, I refused to give up on love. Shortly after my divorce, I manifested the relationship that I knew I deserved. I envisioned a partnership that may not be perfect but would align with my desires. My new husband proposed to me in Rome, and we were married in Venice two years later. When I underwent brain surgery six months into our marriage, he stood by my side. For me, a supportive partner who is by your side in good times as well as challenging times is the ultimate luxury.

After my surgery in 2022, I felt a calling to serve at a higher level. During my recovery, which was at the exact time the world was in a pandemic, I decided to embark on a heart-centered and purpose-driven path. This led me to become a transformational life and love strategist, speaker, and luxury matchmaker because I truly believe in the power of love at the highest level, beginning with self. In this heart-centered space, I have also attracted abundance. I earned six figures in just seven days and built a seven-figure business within 12 months by using my journey as a roadmap to attract abundance.

My Success

Throughout my life, I have faced moments of self-doubt and hopelessness, but I never gave up. I understood the importance of having an open heart, and an open mind and practicing forgiveness. I also maintained an abundance mindset, focusing on gratitude for the things I have overcome and the blessings in my life.

My approach to life is to always look forward to the future and not dwell on a painful past. My goal on this journey is to help you overcome any obstacles that have hindered your desired dreams so you can create a life of luxury on your terms, unapologetically.

The Power of DIVA

I created a framework called DIVA. The Power of D.I.V.A. is my model using 4 keys to attract what you desire. You can create a road map for whatever outcome you want to achieve, whether it's a new career, relationship, more income, or a new home. By implementing these 4 keys and taking action, you can attract the exact kind of luxury you want.

The four keys are **D**esire, **I**nvest, **V**alue, and **A**lign. I will break them down into further detail, and then illustrate how using these keys together can help you achieve your desired outcomes. These can be implemented time and time again.

Desire

Having a strong desire for something or a specific outcome means that you deeply long for it. It could be a goal, an object, or even a feeling that you wish to experience. For example, you may desire to improve your health by eating nutritious food or to shed some weight. Alternatively, you might desire to learn a new skill. Your desires represent what you want in life, aiming for a better and more fulfilling existence.

INVEST

Investing in your personal growth involves taking deliberate steps and making conscious decisions to become a better version of yourself. This investment can be personal, financial, or both. For instance, if you desire to lose weight, you can invest in a gym membership, hire a personal trainer, or commit to a daily morning run. Having a desire or goal is important, but it is equally essential to have a stake in the game, indicating your investment.

VALUE

Valuing yourself at the highest level means recognizing your worth and treating yourself with the love and respect you deserve. It involves understanding that you are deserving of all the things and outcomes you desire. Valuing yourself requires self-work, where you actively increase your self-worth to attract what you want. Techniques such as creating a vision board, practicing positive affirmations daily, reading uplifting stories or quotes, and engaging in positive self-talk can help. I find it helpful to write sticky notes that motivate me and place them on my laptop, mirror, and other visible spots as a constant reminder of my worthiness and aspirations.

ALIGN

Aligning yourself with the right people and environments is crucial for attracting your desired outcomes. This means taking risks, stepping out of your comfort zone, and taking action towards your goals. Staying isolated at home and avoiding interactions with others will not align you with your desires. Similarly, spending time with individuals who devalue what you hold sacred will hinder your progress. It doesn't matter if these individuals are close family members; if their words and actions do not align with your goals, it is essential to seek alignment with like-minded individuals who are striving for similar things or have already achieved what you desire.

By incorporating these four keys into your life, you can unlock the door to your desired outcomes. Remember, desire fuels your motivation, investment propels your growth, valuing yourself attracts what you want, and aligning yourself with the right people and settings sets you on the path to success. Embrace these keys, apply them consistently, and watch as they transform your life time and time again.

Manifest Your Greatness

By using the DIVA model, with your desires and investing in your personal growth, you can create a strong sense of self-worth and value. This, in turn, allows you to align your goals with your true purpose, and attract the things that you desire into your life. By valuing yourself and believing in your ability to achieve your dreams, you can create a powerful energy that draws opportunities and abundance toward you. By focusing on these practices consistently, you can create a life that is aligned with your true desires and purpose.

In conclusion, attracting luxury is about creating a life that is aligned with your true desires and purpose. We have explored the power of manifestation and the law of attraction in bringing your goals and dreams into reality. We have also introduced the DIVA model, which consists of the keys of Desire, Invest, Value, and Align, as a roadmap to attracting what you desire and deserve.

By implementing these keys and taking consistent action, you can create a life filled with abundance and fulfillment.

Remember, attracting luxury is not about luck or chance, but about consciously creating the life you desire. It requires belief in yourself, a positive mindset, and a willingness to take action. Embrace the power of the DIVA model and watch as it transforms your life time and time again. You deserve nothing less than the luxury and fulfillment that you desire.

Part III
Enjoying Luxury With No Apologies

Are you ready? In the final section of this book, we will explore the internal and external practices that will empower you to embrace your newfound life of luxury unapologetically, free from the need to please others.

Chapter 7

THE PRINCIPLES OF LUXURY

"Love is not about possession. Love is about appreciation." – Osho

It's time to move to the next level. You've made your mind up to live an abundant-filled life, and now it's time to walk in it.

The fundamental principles of living the luxurious life that we desire and deserve our includes self-worth, self-value, self-love, setting boundaries, and gratitude. All of those aspects work together for our good. Once we take care of our own lives in those aspects, then it enables us to embody luxury in everything that we do and live unapologetically.

In this chapter, we will explore the interconnected concepts of self-worth, self-value, self-love, and gratitude, which are essential pillars of embodying luxury, which includes personal fulfillment and a genuinely luxurious existence.

Self-First

Just like in the event of a safety situation on an airplane, you are instructed to take care of yourself first, then those close to you. If you are not putting yourself first, you are no good to anyone else. In luxury living, there is a trifecta of concepts that hold immense power: self-worth, self-value, and self-love. While often used interchangeably, these three pillars position us to live in luxury and embody luxury by being an example and helping others.

Self-Worth

First is self-worth. Self-worth encompasses the profound sense of value and significance that resonates within us. It is an internal compass that guides us towards embracing our true selves. It transcends external circumstances, allowing us to recognize our inherent worthiness regardless of the world's judgments. By recognizing our worth and treating ourselves with care, we elevate our self-esteem and confidence.

SELF-VALUE

On the other hand, self-value is recognizing and appreciating our unique qualities, skills, and achievements. It is the unwavering belief that we possess something extraordinary to offer the world, deserving of respect and recognition. By acknowledging our worth, we pave the way for a life of luxury and fulfillment. This leads us to exercise our skills in the lives of others.

SELF-LOVE

Lastly, self-love is the pinnacle of our journey towards a luxurious existence. It entails embracing ourselves unconditionally, flaws and imperfections included. Through acts of kindness, compassion, and forgiveness towards ourselves, we prioritize our own needs and well-being. Self-love is the key that unlocks the door to a life of abundance and contentment. It is the self-love that we have which enables us to love others.

Self-love is when you cherish every aspect of yourself, the good, the bad, and the ugly. You do not shy away from acknowledging your weaknesses, nor do you fear vulnerability. You strive to improve what you can and confidently accept what cannot be changed. Self-love is loving yourself at the highest level and celebrating your accomplishments without seeking validation from others. This unwavering self-love is non-negotiable as you walk in luxury. You love yourself and accept yourself, recognizing that the love you extend to others can only match your love for yourself. And that is at its highest level.

As we embrace self-love, it benefits others. We become catalysts for positive change, empowering others to love themselves and live authentically. Our journey of self-love and personal growth becomes a source of inspiration and encouragement for those around us.

To embark on the path of luxury living, it is crucial to affirm our self-love, self-value, and self-worth. By taking the time to recognize and honor our unique qualities, strengths, and accomplishments, we lay the foundation for a grander existence. Let go of the shackles of perfectionism and embrace every facet of your being, for it is the mosaic of your individuality that sets you apart.

Let Your Voice Use You

Another powerful tool in affirming our self-value and worth is the art of self-talk. Our inner voice can either propel us towards greatness or hinder our progress. Instead of succumbing to doubt and negative beliefs because you are experiencing this new luxury life, reframe your thoughts with empowering affirmations such as "I am worthy" or "I am enough." By rewiring our internal dialogue, we pave the way for a life of luxury and self-fulfillment.

In addition to introspection and affirmations, our worthiness can be demonstrated through action. Start by learning to say no when necessary and prioritizing your physical health. These seemingly insignificant steps will gradually build your confidence and reinforce your belief in your worthiness.

Embodying Luxury As A Person

In our discussions, we explored the multifaceted nature of luxury, encompassing both material possessions and the emotions they evoke. The third part of luxury surpasses all others - embodying luxury as a person. To truly embody luxury is to become a person of immeasurable worth, someone who cherishes their essence and exudes regality with every stride. It is about embracing your true self, acknowledging the trials and triumphs that have shaped you, and harnessing the power to transform pain into purpose.

Your achievements are not merely a result of hard work and dedication; they are a testament to your brilliance and integrity. You do not conceal your imperfections beneath designer garments or layers of makeup; instead, you refine them through introspection, prayer, compassion, and self-care. Your beauty emanates from the depths of your being, intertwining seamlessly with your body, mind, and soul.

By embodying luxury, you become a living embodiment of opulence, radiating an aura of grace and refinement. You are a symbol of elegance, not defined by material possessions alone, but by the richness of your character and the depth of your spirit. Your presence commands attention, captivating all those fortunate enough to cross your path. You shine bright like a diamond from the inside out.

In this pursuit of embodying luxury, you transcend the superficial and embrace a profound sense of self-worth. You recognize that true luxury lies not in the external trappings, but in the cultivation of inner richness. It is a journey of self-discovery, self-love, and self-expression, where you celebrate your uniqueness and embrace the beauty of your individuality.

As you embody luxury, you inspire others to do the same. Your presence becomes a catalyst for transformation, encouraging those around you to embrace their worth and strive for greatness. You become a beacon of light, illuminating the path toward a life of abundance, fulfillment, and genuine luxury.

So, let us embark on this journey together, embracing the essence of luxury as individuals. Let us cultivate our inner radiance, refine our imperfections, and celebrate the beauty that resides within us. For when we embody luxury as people, we transcend the ordinary and step into a realm of extraordinary opulence. We not only transform our own lives but also inspire those around us to do the same. Our actions and choices have a ripple effect, spreading positivity and empowerment to others. Moreover, practicing gratitude is another essential aspect of embodying luxury.

GRATITUDE

To fully embody luxury, it takes gratitude for what we have to push us forward during difficult challenges. As we discussed early on in the book, when we practice gratitude, we take the time to acknowledge and appreciate the blessings in our lives, no matter how big or small. It could be something as simple as having a roof over our heads or a loving family. By recognizing and being grateful for these things, we cultivate a sense of contentment and fulfillment. This helps us to still move forward during difficult times because we can find gratitude in everything good or bad.

Practicing gratitude also helps us develop a positive mindset. Instead of focusing on what we lack or what is going wrong, we train our minds to seek out the positive aspects of every situation. This shift in perspective allows us to find joy and beauty even in challenging circumstances.

Gratitude is also essential in relationships. Expressing gratitude towards others strengthens our relationships. When we show appreciation for the people in our lives, we let them know that we value and cherish their presence. Showing gratitude for the people in our lives also means supporting their endeavors, showing up when they need us, checking in on them, and being trustworthy confidants. Gratitude prevents us from taking others for granted and living with regret later. Gratitude fosters deeper connections and encourages a cycle of kindness and appreciation.

Lastly, gratitude has a significant impact on our overall well-being. Research has shown that regularly practicing gratitude can reduce stress, improve sleep quality, and enhance mental and emotional resilience. It reminds us to focus on the present moment and find happiness in the little things that often go unnoticed.

In a world that often emphasizes what we lack, practicing gratitude is a powerful antidote. It reminds us to count our blessings, no matter how small they seem. Let us make gratitude a daily practice, intentionally cultivating it in our lives. By doing so, we can navigate life's challenges with a grateful heart, finding peace and joy along the way.

LIVING THE LUXURY LIFE

In conclusion, living a luxurious life is not just about material possessions or external trappings. It is about embracing our self-worth, self-value, and self-love, setting boundaries, and practicing gratitude. By prioritizing ourselves and recognizing our inherent worthiness, we lay the foundation for a life of luxury and fulfillment. Embodying luxury as individuals allows us to radiate grace, refinement, and inner richness. It inspires others to embrace their worth and strive for greatness. Through the practice of gratitude, we find contentment, develop a positive mindset, strengthen relationships, and enhance our overall well-being. So, let us embark on this journey of living a luxurious life, embracing our true selves, and spreading positivity and empowerment to others.

Chapter 8

THE UNAPOLOGETIC LIFE

"To be beautiful means to be yourself. You don't need to be accepted by others. You need to accept yourself." -**Thich Nhat Hanh**

Living a luxurious life means embodying luxury in every aspect of your existence. It is not about being a people pleaser but prioritizing your needs and then considering how to benefit the important people in your life. However, it is important to recognize that you cannot please everyone. The key is to know yourself and be intentional in your relationships with others. By doing great things and expecting great things in return, you can live unapologetically, even in the face of significant challenges like loss. Now, let's discuss how to be unapologetic about living a luxurious life.

BE UNAPOLOGETIC

Embracing a luxurious life means fully owning it. It involves loving yourself unconditionally, setting standards and boundaries that benefit yourself and others, and being committed to achieving greatness. When you embody luxury, there is no need to apologize or have regrets because you are living authentically and intentionally. You understand the value of self-worth and prioritize your well-being while also positively impacting those around you. By embracing luxury, you are empowered to live a life without apologies, fully embracing the opportunities and experiences that you deserve.

I often encounter accomplished women who have attained great success through their education and hard work. These women utilize their talents to assist others in achieving their own goals. However, they often find themselves apologizing unnecessarily.

When I mention apologizing, I do not mean expressing remorse for one's achievements. Instead, I am addressing the tendency to downplay one's success to make others who are less accomplished feel more comfortable. Genuine assistance and support for others require us to be honest and unafraid of how our achievements may make them feel. By revealing our true selves, we allow them to witness the face of success and inspire them to strive for more.

LIVE UNAPOLOGETICALLY

When you govern your life with love, integrity, respect, and compassion for others, what do you have to apologize for?

When you embody luxury, you are gentle with yourself and loving with others. Because you embody luxury you can be unapologetic. Being unapologetic means embracing your life and being free of guilt, and regret, apologizing for who you are, or second-guessing your decisions. It also means you refuse to let the opinions or expectations of others hold you back from the peace and freedom you deserve because you know who you are and the positive impact you make on others. When you stand up for your beliefs, live authentically, and are committed to putting good in the world, then good is what you know you will get back to enjoy the luxury of being unapologetic. Being unapologetic doesn't mean you are overly cocky, but you are confident because you live your life intentionally.

Apologizing for who you are, what you have, and what you do is a disservice to yourself. It is crucial to always strive to do your best, but it is equally important to prioritize yourself. Many individuals in corporate settings, for instance, may work long hours and hesitate to take their paid vacations. Even if they take time off, they continue to check in and remain consumed by work. But who are they cheating? When you embody luxury, you give your all to everything you do. As a result, the work you do is exceptional, and it is perfectly acceptable to take a break. Apologizing in this context means feeling compelled to work when you shouldn't, allowing others who never take vacations to make you feel guilty for doing so. We have already discussed the significance of self-care, so remember to prioritize it.

Apologizing for embodying luxury is an oxymoron because not only are you committed to your goals and desires, but you are also dedicated to being an example for others. Luxury brings peace and freedom because you are doing the right things. This grants you the freedom and peace to take a break, for self-care, and to focus on yourself.

Stop apologizing and revel in the freedom of luxury. If you are unable to attend every bridal shower or birthday party due to being honored or receiving an award, do not apologize. If you need to skip a family outing to prioritize self-care and meditation, simply say, "No, I won't be there, but I hope to see you next time." You do not owe anyone an explanation for your need to spend time alone. You have the right to prioritize your own needs. No more apologizing! Embracing a life of luxury means soaring to new heights. Those who understand this, are great. Those who do not, are also great. Others do not define or dictate your life. You do.

When you embody luxury, you expect to experience the tranquility and liberation that luxury offers, including during planned vacations and even in grief.

LUXURY AND LOSS

In the face of adversity and loss, I have discovered the power of unapologetic luxury and the profound gratitude it brings to my life. Despite experiencing the departure of significant individuals, I have chosen to focus on the blessings they got and the cherished moments we shared without any regrets. By embodying a life of luxury, I have made deliberate decisions that hold meaning, allowing me to avoid the burden of remorse.

The sudden passing of my mother in 2022 left me bewildered, unsure of how to navigate the practical aspects of her departure, such as handling her life insurance and settling her affairs. However, a sense of peace prevailed within me, fueled by my gratitude for being an integral part of her life. As her daughter-mom, she trusted and valued my opinions, and I took solace in knowing that I had consistently provided her with love, care, and support. Even in her absence, I embraced the luxury of life, unburdened by regrets. While her loss deeply saddened me, I found comfort in knowing I had fulfilled my role in her life, experiencing the freedom and peace that true luxury brings.

A year later, my father also passed away. Having learned from the experience of losing my mother, I was better prepared to handle the practicalities surrounding my father's departure. As I witnessed his health deteriorate, I ensured that I had access to his important documents and became his healthcare proxy, bringing him comfort in knowing that I would take care of his needs. Although I was not as close to my father, he and my mother were divorced for more than 30 years, I still maintained a relationship with him where he understood that I would always be there when he needed me. Once I discovered that he was ill, I became an active participant in his life, accompanying him to doctor's appointments and embodying luxury in how I cared for him. This mindset allowed me to continue embracing luxury even after his passing, which has left me with tremendous gratitude rather than grief. I celebrated the lives of my parents when they were alive and when they departed.

LEARNING AFTER LOSS

Losses, though painful, have the potential to foster personal growth. Through the experience of losing my mother, I gained valuable insights that prepared me to assist my father during his decline. Each loss has taught me the importance of reflection and alignment, leading me to discover the value of unapologetic living. When we recognize our intrinsic goodness and align with our values, we can fully embody luxury without hesitation. It is in finding gratitude for the simple things in life that we experience peace and intentional gratitude, becoming an integral part of who we are as individuals.

During my journey, I also faced the heart-wrenching loss of my dear cousins, who were more like siblings because they were my mother's twin sister's children. They were both killed in a tragic car accident. This further emphasized embracing peace and intentional gratitude as a luxury. It is through these emotions, experiences, and embodiment that we find the true essence of luxury. Reflecting on our lives and aligning ourselves with what truly matters allows us to tap into the unapologetic nature of luxury, where we place value on the lives of those we love more than things.

To authentically enjoy luxury after loss, it is essential to navigate the practical aspects with knowledge and preparedness. Understanding the responsibilities of being an executor, handling life insurance, and knowing what steps to take are crucial in ensuring a smooth transition. By learning from my experiences with my mother and father, I have gained the wisdom to face these challenges head-on, making things easier and honoring their legacies.

In conclusion, unapologetic luxury can be found even in the face of loss. By embracing gratitude, reflection, and alignment, we can experience the profound peace and intentional gratitude that luxury brings. Through these principles, we discover the intrinsic luxury of appreciating the important people in life.

Let us continue to navigate the practical aspects of luxury with living without regrets and with preparedness. This will enable us to maintain peace and embrace unapologetic luxury amidst life's challenges and losses.

Chapter 9

EMBRACE YOUR LUXURIOUS LIFE

> *"If you are always trying to be normal, you will never know how amazing you can be."* - **Maya Angelou**

You have a luxurious life and are unapologetic, now what?

As you progress to the next level, new challenges may arise triggered by your growth. Embrace the discomfort of growth, knowing it is a sign of progress. Accept the changes that come with leveling up and trust in your ability to navigate them. With dedication, consistency, and a commitment to living your best life, you will overcome these challenges and continue moving toward the abundant life you deserve.

DEDICATION

Dedicating yourself to a life of luxury means taking full ownership of your journey embracing all the incredible opportunities it presents and moving forward. By dedicating yourself to becoming the best version of yourself, you're committing to your growth and development, taking the necessary steps to live your most fulfilling life. Countless inspiring women have committed to personal growth, from Maya Angelou to Michelle Obama, Gloria Steinem to Oprah Winfrey. Now it's your turn.

Dedicating yourself to living in luxury may involve letting go of old habits or beliefs that no longer serve you and embracing new ones that align with your new path. It's about taking a courageous leap toward attracting and owning the life you desire and deserve. Whether it's personal or professional growth, the key to success lies in dedicating yourself to developing self-confidence and embracing all that life has to offer. It takes bravery, determination, and perseverance to become your ideal self, but once you commit, you'll never look back. As Mary Engelbreit wisely said, *"Don't look back; you're not going that way."*

Ensure you surround yourself with positive energy and have faith in your decisions, as they pave the way to a fulfilling future. With dedication comes success and endless growth opportunities, so don't limit your potential by giving up. You can do it!

Consistency

Being consistent about the life you desire and deserve will help you achieve your goals and live a truly fulfilling life. Consistency is the key to lasting changes in your habits, routines, and mindset. It means committing to taking small but meaningful steps towards your goals every day, even when it feels challenging or uncomfortable. By being consistent, you build momentum and progress towards living out your dreams.

By combining consistency with a fearless mindset, you create an unstoppable force that propels you towards your luxurious life. You become confident in yourself, committed to positive changes, and bold in pursuing your dreams. So, once again, be consistent and fearless- the world needs more people who are brave enough to live their best lives and embrace their next-level selves. Countless friends and family have told me I've inspired them to dream bigger. They've witnessed my challenges, but they've also seen me shine and embrace life with confidence, ease, and fearlessness.

As you become your most fabulous self, those around you will notice a change. Some will respond favorably, while others may not. Often, our growth makes certain people uncomfortable, but remember, as you continue this journey, do not be distracted. Stay confident, consistent, and committed to living your luxurious life. You deserve it.

COMMITTING TO THE NEW YOU!

Stepping into your next level of life requires confidence that may feel like you've tapped into an alter ego. This alter ego is a version of yourself that is more self-assured, assertive, and fearless than your everyday self.

Embrace this next level of confidence. By embodying this alter ego, you can overcome self-doubt or fear that may have held you back before and approach challenges more confidently and determinedly.

Know this, your alter ego is still a part of you, not a separate entity. You are simply accessing a different side of yourself that you may not always show. So, don't be afraid to embrace this confidence and let it guide you towards achieving your goals and living your best life.

BUILDING NEXT-LEVEL CONFIDENCE

Building self-confidence and achieving a luxurious life go hand in hand. Here are some ways to achieve the next level of confidence you need to live your best life:

Embrace Triumphs and Trials: Celebrate your victories, but also acknowledge the immense growth you've achieved despite facing challenges and setbacks. Reflecting on your journey not only boosts your confidence but also strengthens your resilience. Remember, personal growth is an ongoing process, and it doesn't have to be flawless. Maintaining a journal is an excellent way to reflect upon your experiences. By documenting and cherishing these accomplishments, you fortify your confidence for future endeavors. Often, successful individuals quickly move on to their next pursuit after achieving a goal. However, to truly relish and embrace the new version of yourself, it's crucial to celebrate your wins and learn from the obstacles you encounter.

Step out of your comfort zone: Embracing new opportunities, taking calculated risks, and fearlessly embracing your authentic self are essential steps toward building confidence. This doesn't imply subjecting yourself to uncomfortable situations. Instead, prioritize inner peace and follow your intuition. However, if something feels right but triggers discomfort, delve deeper into the source of your unease. Is your ego holding you back, or are old limiting beliefs resurfacing? To confidently step out of your comfort zone, you must discern reality from illusion. If your fear stems from the fear of embarrassment, recognize it as mere fear and investigate its origins to overcome it. Be patient with yourself and acknowledge the progress you make along the way.

Keep the big picture in mind: Living a life of luxury requires time, dedication, and unwavering perseverance. Believe in yourself and remember that building confidence is an ongoing journey. The bigger picture encompasses the freedom and abundance your luxurious life will bring, both now and in the future. As you progress to the next level, new challenges may arise, often internal ones triggered by change. To get to your destination, don't make a big deal out of the little difficulties because, in the big scheme of things, it will not matter later.

YOU EMBODY LUXURY!

It's time to step up and embrace the next level of abundance. Stay focused, stay committed, and watch your life transform into the extraordinary. Embrace your luxurious life with unwavering confidence, consistency, and fearlessness. Embody it, own it, and claim it because it is your birthright. You deserve nothing less than the extraordinary. By implementing these strategies, you will elevate your confidence to new heights, unlocking the luxury life that awaits you.

Chapter 10

LUXURY LIFE UNVEILED

"A Luxury Mindset with gratitude knows that true opulence is in appreciating every refined moment." **-Dr. Felisha Kay**

It's time to enter a world of opulence and extravagance, where luxury becomes your everyday reality. Allow this book to be your trusted companion, leading you towards the life you've always yearned for.

In *Luxury Life Unveiled: Unlocking the Secrets to Attract Your Dream Life with No Apologies*, we delved deep into the significance of self-belief, gracefully accepting our flaws, and nurturing ourselves through self-care and introspection. The initial chapters laid the groundwork for a life of unapologetic luxury, where seeking validation from others becomes irrelevant as we flourish in our magnificence.

Moving forward, we unraveled the true essence of luxury, exploring its profound meaning and revealing the art of preparation. Finally, you learned to embrace your newfound life of luxury without seeking approval from anyone else.

I encouraged you not only to integrate the teachings into your daily existence. Banish negative thoughts and replace them with positive affirmations, self-love, and an abundance mindset. This transformation will unlock your deepest desires, allowing you to attract and manifest your dreams. By fearlessly embracing a life of luxury, you will exude confidence and refuse to apologize for your success.

Surround yourself with like-minded individuals who have already achieved the desires you seek. Instead of viewing them as competition, let their accomplishments inspire you to set even higher goals. By surrounding yourself with greatness, you will bask in the luxury of their presence. Remember, to truly embody luxury, your mind and body must be in perfect harmony, enabling you to enter any room with grace and radiate opulence, inspiring others to embark on their path toward happiness and triumph.

Throughout this journey, prioritizing self-care is crucial to sustain and maintain your luxurious lifestyle. Take the time to relish in the small yet lavish moments of your daily life. Here are some steps to indulge in such luxuries:

Embrace the Pace of Nature: Take a stroll outside and synchronize your heartbeat with the gentle rhythm of nature.

Find Serenity in Stillness: Discover a quiet sanctuary and be simple, even for a few minutes.

Celebrate Your Senses: Delight in local delicacies, inhale the scents of your surroundings and connect with the earth through touch.

Express Gratitude: Each evening, reflect on the day's gifts, no matter how small they may seem.

Cultivate Joy: Engage in activities that ignite your soul each day - read, dance, paint, and sing with the uninhibited spirit of a child.

Let us not merely pass through life but pause to revel in its wonders. Let's immerse ourselves in the constant ebb and flow of life's luxuries.

I am Dr. Felisha Kay, your Luxury Love Diva, and I am here to lead you on this magnificent journey. If you desire to embark on this transformative expedition with me as your guide, then please don't hesitate to reach out.

With love and luxury,

Dr. Felisha Kay

A Luxurious Love Note From The Author

Thank you for purchasing this book. I want you to know that regardless of your credentials or experiences, you deserve the best life possible, and I hope you attain it. Do not allow past trauma to hold you back from the luxurious life that you deserve.

Here's the thing, *"Life will life, but we must persevere and luxuriate."* What I mean by that is, as we move through the terrain of growing pains, navigate the complexities of divorces, bear the weight of losses, adapt to life shifts, embrace pivots, and face a myriad of other challenges, we must never lose sight of the profound gratitude that should permanently reside in our hearts. Take time to luxuriate in self-care without apology. You are worth it. Love yourself as the worthy woman you are. Shine bright like a precious gem, and make no apologies for desiring more. It's your time to sparkle, or as I love to say, *"Be the Diamond in the Room!"*

Keep growing gracefully, showing up enthusiastically, loving deeply, and finding your joy!

Luxuriously Yours,

Dr. Felisha Kay

References

Simone, K. (2022, May 4). *4 easy tips on creating and sticking to a writing schedule*. Medium. https://writingcooperative.com/4-easy-tips-on-creating-and-sticking-to-a-writing-schedule-154793db5a2

Barrero, J. M., Bloom, N., & Davis, S. (2021). Why working from Home Will Stick. *NATIONAL BUREAU OF ECONOMIC RESEARCH, 28731*. https://doi.org/10.3386/w28731

Kay, F. [@luxurylovediva]. (2023, October 25). A luxury mindset paired with gratitude is understanding that the truest form of opulence lies not in what we have [photograph]. https://www.instagram.com/p/CyOO7iFuoPL/?igshid=MzRlODBiNWFlZA==

Kay, F. [@luxurylovediva]. (2023, September 07). Keep valuing yourself at the highest level in life and in love [photograph]. https://www.instagram.com/p/Cw3WRZUOO6g/?igshid=MzRlODBiNWFlZA==

Gilles Marini. (n.d.). *Quotefancy*. https://quotefancy.com/quote/1687332/Gilles-Marini-The-most-important-thing-in-your-life-is-to-be-happy-to-be-patient-and-to

Angelou, M. (n.d.). *Chocolate and Steel.* https://chocolateandsteel.com/products/maya-angelou?variant=39435406213313

Mind Blood. (2021, October 13). *Never settle for less than what you deserve - anonymous.* https://mindblood.com/never-settle-for-less-than-what-you-deserve/

Newswire, I. (2023, July 13). *Here's some tips on building up your self-confidence.* KSAT. https://www.ksat.com/news/2023/07/13/heres-some-tips-on-building-up-your-self-confidence/

Hanh, T. N. (n.d.). *Quotefancy.* https://quotefancy.com/quote/874719/Nhat-Hanh-To-be-beautiful-means-to-be-yourself-You-don-t-need-to-be-accepted-by-others

Maraboli, S. (2023, March 22). *70+ growth mindset quotes about hard work and perseverance.* We Are Teachers. https://www.weareteachers.com/growth-mindset-quotes/

Osho. (2017, January 25). *Love: Appreciation vs possession & why possessiveness is toxic in any relationship.* Medium. https://medium.com/@MichealSinclair/love-appreciation-vs-possession-why-possessiven ess-is-toxic-in-any-relationship-7239bb480811

Ball, L. (2017, March 9). The Swerve. https://theswerve187.com/2017/03/09/inspirational-quotes-from-inspirational-females-by-leo-l-701/

Forbes. M. S. (n.d.). *PoetrySoup.com.* https://www.poetrysoup.com/famous/quote/82599_too_many_people_overvalue_what_th

Weingus, L. (2022, January 11). *52 quotes that will remind you not to settle for less.* Silk + Sonder. https://www.silkandsonder.com/blogs/news/52-quotes-that-will-remind-you-not-to-settle-for-less

Author Bio

Dr. Felisha Kay, also known as The Luxury Love Diva, is an award-winning Entrepreneur, Luxury Love Strategist, and luxury matchmaker. She lives between the United States and Costa Rica where she luxuriates in peace and tranquility. Embracing a luxury mindset, Dr. Felisha Kay is a true manifestation expert and a beacon of abundance attraction.

Dr. Felisha Kay embarked on her journey with the triumphant launch of her first business at the age of nineteen. The subsequent sale of this venture for a remarkable sum not only marked a significant achievement but also laid the foundation for her future endeavors. This early success became the catalyst that fueled Felisha's unwavering drive to make a meaningful difference.

Dr. Felisha Kay is a Domestic Violence Survivor who has chosen to live an empowered life. In 1996, she founded one of the largest online support communities for victims and survivors of Domestic Violence. This initiative gained global recognition and earned Felisha a prestigious Women of Excellence Award. She was also named Entrepreneur of the Year by NAFE (National Association for Female Executives), which further solidified her commitment to helping others.

Dr. Felisha Kay is no stranger to higher education and pursuing her dreams rooted in Beauty and Science at, the University of Denver. She is a Cosmetic Chemist and Fine Fragrance Artist/Perfumer. . She also holds a Ph.D. in Business. Driven by her passion for fragrance, Felisha is an Internationally trained Perfumer. She gained skills taught from renowned institutions based in Thailand and Grasse, France, known as the birthplace of modern perfumery. Felisha's commitment to personal and professional growth is evident. She has several certifications, including science-based coaching, and is a recognized member of the Society of Cosmetic Chemists. Furthermore, she has achieved the esteemed Master Matchmaker showcasing her ability to bring people together and foster meaningful partnerships in life and love.

As an author, Dr. Felisha Kay shares her wealth of knowledge and experience to empower women to present the best version of themselves and discover the unparalleled peace and freedom that accompanies a life of unapologetic luxury. Beyond her professional accomplishments, Felisha is a devoted wife, mother, and compassionate voice to all. Her dedication to making a positive impact in the lives of others is truly inspiring.

Author Contact Information:

Website:

https://felishakay.com

Social Media:

https://instagram.com/luxurylovediva

https://www.facebook.com/luxurylovediva

http://www.linkin.com/in/felishakay

http://www.youtube.com/@felishakay

www.ingramcontent.com/pod-product-compliance
Lightning Source LLC
Chambersburg PA
CBHW051945160426
43198CB00013B/2304